Forming Consciences

for

Faithful Citizenship

A Call to Political Responsibility
from the Catholic Bishops
of the United States

United States Conference of Catholic Bishops • Washington, D.C.

The document *Forming Consciences for Faithful Citizenship: A Call to Political Responsibility* from the Catholic bishops of the United States was developed by the chairmen, in consultation with the membership, of the Committees on Domestic Policy, International Policy, Pro-Life Activities, Communications, Doctrine, Education, and Migration of the United States Conference of Catholic Bishops (USCCB). It was approved by the full body of bishops at its November 2007 General Meeting and has been authorized for publication by the undersigned.

Msgr. David J. Malloy, STD
General Secretary, USCCB

Photos: pp. iv, 24, Blend Images, LLC; pp. 5, 11, 27, Digital Vision; p. 6, Doug J. Hall; p. 15, © Ron Chapple Stock/Corbis; p. 16, Reuters/Ceerwan Aziz; p. 18, Reuters/Mark Wilson; p. 21, Sassy Stock; p. 28, Stockbyte; p. 29, © Corbis/vol 70 Washington D.C.

Scripture texts used in this work are taken from the *New American Bible,* copyright © 1991, 1986, and 1970 by the Confraternity of Christian Doctrine, Washington, DC 20017 and are used by permission of the copyright owner. All rights reserved.

Excerpts from the *Catechism of the Catholic Church*, second edition, copyright © 2000, Libreria Editrice Vaticana–United States Conference of Catholic Bishops, Washington, D.C. Used with permission. All rights reserved.

First printing, November 2007

ISBN: 978-1-60137-026-6

contents

faithful citizenship

PART I

Forming Consciences for Faithful Citizenship: The U.S. Bishops' Reflection on Catholic Teaching and Political Life

Introduction

1. As a nation, we share many blessings and strengths, including a tradition of religious freedom and political participation. However, as a people, we face serious challenges that are clearly political and also profoundly moral.

2. We are a nation founded on "life, liberty, and the pursuit of happiness," but the right to life itself is not fully protected, especially for unborn children, the most vulnerable members of the American family. We are called to be peacemakers in a nation at war. We are a country pledged to pursue "liberty and justice for all," but we are too often divided across lines of race, ethnicity, and economic inequality. We are a nation of immigrants, struggling to address the challenges of many new immigrants in our midst. We are a society built on the strength of our families, called to defend marriage and offer moral and economic supports for family life. We are a powerful nation in a violent world, confronting terror and trying to build a safer, more just, more peaceful world. We are an affluent society where too many live in poverty and lack health care and other necessities of life. We are part of a global community facing urgent threats to the environment that must sustain us. These challenges are at the heart of public life and at the center of the pursuit of the common good.[1]

3. For many years, we bishops of the United States have sought to share Catholic teaching on political life. We have done so in a series of statements issued every four years focused on "political responsibility" or "faithful citizenship." In this document we continue that practice, maintaining continuity with what we have

said in the past in light of new challenges facing our nation and world. This is not new teaching but affirms what is taught by our Bishops' Conference and the whole Church. As Catholics, we are part of a community with a rich heritage that helps us consider the challenges in public life and contribute to greater justice and peace for all people.

4. Part of that rich heritage on faithful citizenship is the teaching of Vatican Council II's *Declaration on Religious Liberty* (*Dignitatis Humanae*). It says that "society itself may enjoy the benefits of justice and peace, which result from [people's] faithfulness to God and his holy will" (no. 6). The work for justice requires that the mind and the heart of Catholics be educated and formed to know and practice the whole faith.

5. This statement highlights the role of the Church in the formation of conscience, and the corresponding moral responsibility of each Catholic to hear, receive, and act upon the Church's teaching in the lifelong task of forming his or her own conscience. With this foundation, Catholics are better able to evaluate policy positions, party platforms, and candidates' promises and actions in light of the Gospel and the moral and social teaching of the Church in order to help build a better world.

6. We seek to do this by addressing four questions: (1) Why does the Church teach about issues affecting public policy? (2) Who in the Church should participate in political life? (3) How does the Church help the Catholic faithful to speak about political and social questions? (4) What does the Church say about Catholic social teaching in the public square?

7. In this statement, we bishops do not intend to tell Catholics for whom or against whom to vote. Our purpose is to help Catholics form their consciences in accordance with God's truth. We recognize that the responsibility to make choices in political life rests with each individual in light of a properly formed conscience, and that participation goes well beyond casting a vote in a particular election.

> **The work for justice requires that the mind and the heart of Catholics be educated and formed to know and practice the whole faith.**

8. During election years, there may be many handouts and voter guides that are produced and distributed. We encourage Catholics to seek those resources that are authorized by their own bishops, their state Catholic conferences, and the United States Conference of Catholic Bishops. This statement is intended to reflect and complement, not substitute for, the ongoing teaching of bishops in our own dioceses and states. In light of these reflections and those of local bishops, we encourage Catholics throughout the United States to be active in the political process, particularly in these challenging times.

Why Does the Church Teach About Issues Affecting Public Policy?

9. The Church's obligation to participate in shaping the moral character of society is a requirement of our faith. It is a basic part of the mission we have received from Jesus Christ, who offers a vision of life revealed to us in Sacred Scripture and Tradition. To echo the teaching of the Second Vatican Council: Christ, the Word made flesh, in showing us the Father's love, also shows us what it truly means to be human (see *Gaudium et Spes*, no. 22). Christ's love for us lets us see our human dignity in full clarity and compels us to love our neighbors as he has loved us. Christ, the Teacher, shows us what is true and good, that is, what is in accord with our human nature as free, intelligent beings created in God's image and likeness and endowed by the Creator with dignity and rights.

10. What faith teaches about the dignity of the human person and about the sacredness of every human life helps us see more clearly the same truths that also come to us through the gift of human reason. At the center of these truths is respect for the dignity of every person. This is the core of Catholic moral and social teaching. Because we are people of both faith and reason, it is appropriate and necessary for us to bring this essential truth about human life and dignity to the public square. We are called to practice Christ's commandment to "love one another" (Jn 13:34). We are also called to promote the well-being of all, to share our blessings with those most in need, to defend marriage, and to protect the lives and dignity of all, especially the weak, the vulnerable, the voiceless. In his first encyclical letter, *Deus Caritas Est*, Pope Benedict XVI explained that "charity must animate the entire lives of the lay faithful and therefore also their political activity, lived as 'social charity'" (no. 29).

11. Some question whether it is appropriate for the Church to play a role in political life. However, the obligation to teach about moral values that should shape our lives, including our public lives, is central to the mission given to the Church by Jesus Christ. Moreover, the United States Constitution protects the

right of individual believers and religious bodies to participate and speak out without government interference, favoritism, or discrimination. Civil law should fully recognize and protect the Church's right, obligation, and opportunities to participate in society without being forced to abandon or ignore its central moral convictions. Our nation's tradition of pluralism is enhanced, not threatened, when religious groups and people of faith bring their convictions and concerns into public life. Indeed, our Church's teaching is in accord with the foundational values that have shaped our nation's history: "life, liberty, and the pursuit of happiness."

12. The Catholic community brings important assets to the political dialogue about our nation's future. We bring a consistent moral framework—drawn from basic human reason that is illuminated by Scripture and the teaching of the Church—for assessing issues, political platforms, and campaigns. We also bring broad experience in serving those in need—educating the young, caring for the sick, sheltering the homeless, helping women who face difficult pregnancies, feeding the hungry, welcoming immigrants and refugees, reaching out in global solidarity, and pursuing peace.

Who in the Church Should Participate in Political Life?

13. In the Catholic Tradition, responsible citizenship is a virtue, and participation in political life is a moral obligation. This obligation is rooted in our baptismal commitment to follow Jesus Christ and to bear Christian witness in all we do. As the *Catechism of the Catholic Church* reminds us, "It is necessary that all participate, each according to his position and role, in promoting the common good. This obligation is inherent in the dignity of the human person. . . . As far as possible citizens should take an active part in public life" (nos. 1913-1915).

14. Unfortunately, politics in our country often can be a contest of powerful interests, partisan attacks, sound bites, and media hype. The Church calls for a different kind of political engagement: one shaped by the moral convictions of well-formed consciences and focused on the dignity of every human being, the pursuit of the common good, and the protection of the weak and the vulnerable. The Catholic call to faithful citizenship affirms the importance of political participation and insists that public service is a worthy vocation. As Catholics, we should be guided more by our moral convictions than by our attachment to a political party or interest group. When necessary, our participation should help transform the party to which we belong; we should not let the party transform us in such a way that we neglect or deny fundamental moral truths. We are called to bring together our principles and our political choices, our values and our votes, to help build a better world.

4

15. Clergy and lay people have complementary roles in public life. We bishops have the primary responsibility to hand on the Church's moral and social teaching. Together with priests and deacons, assisted by religious and lay leaders of the Church, we are to teach fundamental moral principles that help Catholics form their consciences correctly, to provide guidance on the moral dimensions of public decisions, and to encourage the faithful to carry out their responsibilities in political life. In fulfilling these responsibilities, the Church's leaders are to avoid endorsing or opposing candidates or telling people how to vote. As Pope Benedict XVI stated in *Deus Caritas Est,*

> The Church wishes to help form consciences in political life and to stimulate greater insight into the authentic requirements of justice as well as greater readiness to act accordingly, even when this might involve conflict with situations of personal interest. . . . The Church cannot and must not take upon herself the political battle to bring about the most just society possible. She cannot and must not replace the State. Yet at the same time she cannot and must not remain on the sidelines in the fight for justice. (no. 28)

16. As the Holy Father also taught in *Deus Caritas Est,* "The direct duty to work for a just ordering of society is proper to the lay faithful" (no. 29). This duty is

more critical than ever in today's political environment, where Catholics may feel politically disenfranchised, sensing that no party and too few candidates fully share the Church's comprehensive commitment to the life and dignity of every human being from conception to natural death. Yet this is not a time for retreat or discouragement; rather, it is a time for renewed engagement. Forming their consciences in accord with Catholic teaching, Catholic lay women and men can become actively involved: running for office; working within political parties; communicating their concerns and positions to elected officials; and joining diocesan social mission or advocacy networks, state Catholic conference initiatives, community organizations, and other efforts to apply authentic moral teaching in the public square. Even those who cannot vote have the right to have their voices heard on issues that affect their lives and the common good.

How Does the Church Help the Catholic Faithful to Speak About Political and Social Questions?

A Well-Formed Conscience

17. The Church equips its members to address political and social questions by helping them to develop a well-formed conscience. Catholics have a serious and lifelong obligation to form their consciences in accord with human reason and the teaching of the Church. Conscience is not something that allows us to justify doing whatever we want, nor is it a mere "feeling" about what we should or should

not do. Rather, conscience is the voice of God resounding in the human heart, revealing the truth to us and calling us to do what is good while shunning what is evil. Conscience always requires serious attempts to make sound moral judgments based on the truths of our faith. As stated in the *Catechism of the Catholic Church*, "Conscience is a judgment of reason whereby the human person recognizes the moral quality of a concrete act that he is going to perform, is in the process of performing, or has already completed. In all he says and does, man is obliged to follow faithfully what he knows to be just and right" (no. 1778).

18. The formation of conscience includes several elements. First, there is a desire to embrace goodness and truth. For Catholics this begins with a willingness and openness to seek the truth and what is right by studying Sacred Scripture and the teaching of the Church as contained in the *Catechism of the Catholic Church*. It is also important to examine the facts and background information about various choices. Finally, prayerful reflection is essential to discern the will of God. Catholics must also understand that if they fail to form their consciences they can make erroneous judgments.[2]

The Virtue of Prudence

19. The Church fosters well-formed consciences not only by teaching moral truth but also by encouraging its members to develop the virtue of prudence. Prudence enables us "to discern our true good in every circumstance and to choose the right means of achieving it" (*Catechism of the Catholic Church*, no. 1806). Prudence shapes and informs our ability to deliberate over available alternatives, to determine what is most fitting to a specific context, and to act decisively. Exercising this virtue often requires the courage to act in defense of moral principles when making decisions about how to build a society of justice and peace.

20. The Church's teaching is clear that a good end does not justify an immoral means. As we all seek to advance the common good—by defending the inviolable sanctity of human life from the moment of conception until natural death, by defending marriage, by feeding the hungry and housing the homeless, by welcoming the immigrant and protecting the environment—it is important to recognize that not all possible courses of action are morally acceptable. We have a responsibility to discern carefully which public policies are morally sound. Catholics may choose different ways to respond to compelling social problems, but we cannot differ on our moral obligation to help build a more just and peaceful world through morally acceptable means, so that the weak and vulnerable are protected and human rights and dignity are defended.

Doing Good and Avoiding Evil

21. Aided by the virtue of prudence in the exercise of well-formed consciences, Catholics are called to make practical judgments regarding good and evil choices in the political arena.

22. There are some things we must never do, as individuals or as a society, because they are always incompatible with love of God and neighbor. Such actions are so deeply flawed that they are always opposed to the authentic good of persons. These are called "intrinsically evil" actions. They must always be rejected and opposed and must never be supported or condoned. A prime example is the intentional taking of innocent human life, as in abortion and euthanasia. In our nation, "abortion and euthanasia have become preeminent threats to human dignity because they directly attack life itself, the most fundamental human good and the condition for all others" (*Living the Gospel of Life*, no. 5). It is a mistake with grave moral consequences to treat the destruction of innocent human life merely as a matter of individual choice. A legal system that violates the basic right to life on the grounds of choice is fundamentally flawed.

23. Similarly, direct threats to the sanctity and dignity of human life, such as human cloning and destructive research on human embryos, are also intrinsically evil. These must always be opposed. Other direct assaults on innocent human life and violations of human dignity, such as genocide, torture, racism, and the targeting of noncombatants in acts of terror or war, can never be justified.

24. Opposition to intrinsically evil acts that undercut the dignity of the human person should also open our eyes to the good we must do, that is, to our positive duty to contribute to the common good and to act in solidarity with those in need. As Pope John Paul II said, "The fact that only the negative commandments oblige always and under all circumstances does not mean that in the moral life prohibitions are more important than the obligation to do good indicated by the positive commandment" (*Veritatis Splendor*, no. 52). Both opposing evil *and* doing good are essential obligations.

25. The right to life implies and is linked to other human rights—to the basic goods that every human person needs to live and thrive. All the life issues are connected, for erosion of respect for the life of any individual or group in society necessarily diminishes respect for all life. The moral imperative to respond to the needs of our neighbors—basic needs such as food, shelter, health care, education, and meaningful work—is universally binding on our consciences and may be

legitimately fulfilled by a variety of means. Catholics must seek the best ways to respond to these needs. As Blessed Pope John XXIII taught, "[Each of us] has the right to life, to bodily integrity, and to the means which are suitable for the proper development of life; these are primarily food, clothing, shelter, rest, medical care, and, finally, the necessary social services" (*Pacem in Terris*, no. 11).

26. Pope John Paul II explained the importance of being true to fundamental Church teachings:

> Above all, the common outcry, which is justly made on behalf
> of human rights—for example, the right to health, to home,
> to work, to family, to culture—is false and illusory if *the right
> to life*, the most basic and fundamental right and the condition
> for all other personal rights, is not defended with maximum
> determination. (*Christifideles Laici*, no. 38)

27. Two temptations in public life can distort the Church's defense of human life and dignity:

28. The first is a moral equivalence that makes no ethical distinctions between different kinds of issues involving human life and dignity. The direct and intentional destruction of innocent human life from the moment of conception until natural death is always wrong and is not just one issue among many. It must always be opposed.[3]

29. The second is the misuse of these necessary moral distinctions as a way of dismissing or ignoring other serious threats to human life and dignity. Racism and other unjust discrimination, the use of the death penalty, resorting to unjust war, the use of torture,[4] war crimes, the failure to respond to those who are suffering from hunger or a lack of health care, or an unjust immigration policy are all serious moral issues that challenge our consciences and require us to act. These are not optional concerns which can be dismissed. Catholics are urged to seriously consider Church teaching on these issues. Although choices about how best to respond to these and other compelling threats to human life and dignity are matters for principled debate and decision, this does not make them optional concerns or permit Catholics to dismiss or ignore Church teaching on these important issues. Clearly not every Catholic can be actively involved on each of these concerns, but we need to support one another as our community of faith defends human life and dignity wherever it is threatened. We are not factions, but one family of faith fulfilling the mission of Jesus Christ.

30. The Vatican Congregation for the Doctrine of the Faith made a similar point:

> It must be noted also that a well-formed Christian conscience does not permit one to vote for a political program or an individual law which contradicts the fundamental contents of faith and morals. The Christian faith is an integral unity, and thus it is incoherent to isolate some particular element to the detriment of the whole of Catholic doctrine. A political commitment to a single isolated aspect of the Church's social doctrine does not exhaust one's responsibility towards the common good. (*Doctrinal Note on Some Questions Regarding the Participation of Catholics in Political Life*, no. 4)

Making Moral Choices

31. Decisions about political life are complex and require the exercise of a well-formed conscience aided by prudence. This exercise of conscience begins with outright opposition to laws and other policies that violate human life or weaken its protection. Those who knowingly, willingly, and directly support public policies or legislation that undermine fundamental moral principles cooperate with evil.

32. Sometimes morally flawed laws already exist. In this situation, the process of framing legislation to protect life is subject to prudential judgment and "the art of the possible." At times this process may restore justice only partially or gradually. For example, Pope John Paul II taught that when a government official who fully opposes abortion cannot succeed in completely overturning a pro-abortion law, he or she may work to improve protection for unborn human life, "limiting the harm done by such a law" and lessening its negative impact as much as possible (*Evangelium Vitae*, no. 73). Such incremental improvements in the law are acceptable as steps toward the full restoration of justice. However, Catholics must never abandon the moral requirement to seek full protection for all human life from the moment of conception until natural death.

33. Prudential judgment is also needed in applying moral principles to specific policy choices in areas such as the war in Iraq, housing, health care, immigration, and others. This does not mean that all choices are equally valid, or that our guidance and that of other Church leaders is just another political opinion or policy preference among many others. Rather, we urge Catholics to listen carefully to the Church's teachers when we apply Catholic social teaching to specific proposals and situations. The judgments and recommendations that we make as bishops on specific issues do not carry the same moral authority as statements of

universal moral teachings. Nevertheless, the Church's guidance on these matters is an essential resource for Catholics as they determine whether their own moral judgments are consistent with the Gospel and with Catholic teaching.

34. Catholics often face difficult choices about how to vote. This is why it is so important to vote according to a well-formed conscience that perceives the proper relationship among moral goods. A Catholic cannot vote for a candidate who takes a position in favor of an intrinsic evil, such as abortion or racism, if the voter's intent is to support that position. In such cases a Catholic would be guilty of formal cooperation in grave evil. At the same time, a voter should not use a candidate's opposition to an intrinsic evil to justify indifference or inattentiveness to other important moral issues involving human life and dignity.

35. There may be times when a Catholic who rejects a candidate's unacceptable position may decide to vote for that candidate for other morally grave reasons. Voting in this way would be permissible only for truly grave moral reasons, not to advance narrow interests or partisan preferences or to ignore a fundamental moral evil.

36. When all candidates hold a position in favor of an intrinsic evil, the conscientious voter faces a dilemma. The voter may decide to take the extraordinary step of not voting for any candidate or, after careful deliberation, may decide to vote for the candidate deemed less likely to advance such a morally flawed position and more likely to pursue other authentic human goods.

37. In making these decisions, it is essential for Catholics to be guided by a well-formed conscience that recognizes that all issues do not carry the same moral weight and that the moral obligation to oppose intrinsically evil acts has a special claim on our consciences and our actions. These decisions should take into account a candidate's commitments, character, integrity, and ability to influence a given issue.

11

In the end, this is a decision to be made by each Catholic guided by a conscience formed by Catholic moral teaching.

38. It is important to be clear that the political choices faced by citizens not only have an impact on general peace and prosperity but also may affect the individual's salvation. Similarly, the kinds of laws and policies supported by public officials affect their spiritual well-being. Pope Benedict XVI, in his recent reflection on the Eucharist as "the sacrament of charity," challenged all of us to adopt what he calls "a Eucharistic form of life." This means that the redeeming love we encounter in the Eucharist should shape our thoughts, our words, and our decisions, including those that pertain to the social order. The Holy Father called for "Eucharistic consistency" on the part of every member of the Church:

> It is important to consider what the Synod Fathers described as *eucharistic consistency*, a quality which our lives are objectively called to embody. Worship pleasing to God can never be a purely private matter, without consequences for our relationships with others: it demands a public witness to our faith. Evidently, this is true for all the baptized, yet it is especially incumbent upon those who, by virtue of their social or political position, must make decisions regarding fundamental values, such as respect for human life, its defense from conception to natural death, the family built upon marriage between a man and a woman, the freedom to educate one's children and the promotion of the common good in all its forms. . . . (*Sacramentum Caritatis*, no. 83)

39. The Holy Father, in a particular way, called on Catholic politicians and legislators to recognize their grave responsibility in society to support laws shaped by these fundamental human values, and urged them to oppose laws and policies that violate life and dignity at any stage from conception to natural death. He affirmed the responsibility of bishops to teach these values consistently to all of their people.[5]

What Does the Church Say About Catholic Social Teaching in the Public Square?—Seven Key Themes

40. The consistent ethic of life provides a moral framework for principled Catholic engagement in political life and, rightly understood, neither treats all issues as morally equivalent nor reduces Catholic teaching to one or two issues. It anchors the Catholic commitment to defend human life, from conception until natural death, in the fundamental moral obligation to respect the dignity of every person as a child of God. It unites us as a "people of life and for life" (*Evangelium Vitae*, no. 6)

pledged to build what Pope John Paul II called a "culture of life" (*Evangelium Vitae*, no. 77). This culture of life begins with the preeminent obligation to protect innocent life from direct attack and extends to defending life whenever it is threatened or diminished.

41. Catholic voters should use the framework of Catholic teaching to examine candidates' positions on issues affecting human life and dignity as well as issues of justice and peace, and they should consider candidates' integrity, philosophy, and performance. It is important for all citizens "to see beyond party politics, to analyze campaign rhetoric critically, and to choose their political leaders according to principle, not party affiliation or mere self-interest" (*Living the Gospel of Life*, no. 33).

42. As Catholics we are not single-issue voters. A candidate's position on a single issue is not sufficient to guarantee a voter's support. Yet a candidate's position on a single issue that involves an intrinsic evil, such as support for legal abortion or the promotion of racism, may legitimately lead a voter to disqualify a candidate from receiving support.

43. As noted previously, the Catholic approach to faithful citizenship rests on moral principles found in Scripture and Catholic moral and social teaching as well as in the hearts of all people of good will. We now present central and enduring themes of the Catholic social tradition that can provide a moral framework for decisions in public life.[6]

The Right to Life and the Dignity of the Human Person

44. Human life is sacred. The dignity of the human person is the foundation of a moral vision for society. Direct attacks on innocent persons are never morally acceptable, at any stage or in any condition. In our society, human life is especially under direct attack from abortion. Other direct threats to the sanctity of human life include euthanasia, human cloning, and the destruction of human embryos for research.

45. Catholic teaching about the dignity of life calls us to oppose torture,[7] unjust war, and the use of the death penalty; to prevent genocide and attacks against noncombatants; to oppose racism; and to overcome poverty and suffering. Nations are called to protect the right to life by seeking effective ways to combat evil and terror without resorting to armed conflicts except as a last resort, always seeking first to resolve disputes by peaceful means. We revere the lives of children in the womb, the lives of persons dying in war and from starvation, and indeed the lives of all human beings as children of God.

Call to Family, Community, and Participation

46. The human person is not only sacred but also social. Full human development takes place in relationship with others. The family—based on marriage between a man and a woman—is the first and fundamental unit of society and is a sanctuary for the creation and nurturing of children. It should be defended and strengthened, not redefined or undermined by permitting same-sex unions or other distortions of marriage. Respect for the family should be reflected in every policy and program. It is important to uphold parents' rights and responsibilities to care for their children, including the right to choose their children's education.

47. How we organize our society—in economics and politics, in law and policy—directly affects the common good and the capacity of individuals to develop their full potential. Every person and association has a right and a duty to participate actively in shaping society and to promote the well-being of all, especially the poor and vulnerable.

48. The principle of subsidiarity reminds us that larger institutions in society should not overwhelm or interfere with smaller or local institutions, yet larger institutions have essential responsibilities when the more local institutions cannot adequately protect human dignity, meet human needs, and advance the common good.

Rights and Responsibilities

49. Human dignity is respected and the common good is fostered only if human rights are protected and basic responsibilities are met. Every human being has a right to life, the fundamental right that makes all other rights possible, and a right to access to those things required for human decency—food and shelter, education and employment, health care and housing, freedom of religion and family life. The right to exercise religious freedom publicly and privately by individuals and institutions along with freedom of conscience need to be constantly defended. In a fundamental way, the right to free expression of religious beliefs protects all other rights. Corresponding to these rights are duties and responsibilities—to one another, to our families, and to the larger society. Rights should be understood and exercised in a moral framework rooted in the dignity of the human person.

Option for the Poor and Vulnerable

50. While the common good embraces all, those who are weak, vulnerable, and most in need deserve preferential concern. A basic moral test for our society is how we treat the most vulnerable in our midst. In a society marred by deepening disparities between rich and poor, Scripture gives us the story of the Last Judgment

(see Mt 25:31-46) and reminds us that we will be judged by our response to the "least among us." The *Catechism of the Catholic Church* explains:

> Those who are oppressed by poverty are the object of *a preferential love* on the part of the Church which, since her origin and in spite of the failings of many of her members, has not ceased to work for their relief, defense, and liberation through numerous works of charity which remain indispensable always and everywhere. (no. 2448)

51. Pope Benedict XVI has taught that "love for widows and orphans, prisoners, and the sick and needy of every kind, is as essential to [the Church] as the ministry of the sacraments and preaching of the Gospel" (*Deus Caritas Est,* no. 22). This preferential option for the poor and vulnerable includes all who are marginalized in our nation and beyond—unborn children, persons with disabilities, the elderly and terminally ill, and victims of injustice and oppression.

Dignity of Work and the Rights of Workers

52. The economy must serve people, not the other way around. Work is more than a way to make a living; it is a form of continuing participation in God's creation. Employers contribute to the common good through the services or products they

provide and by creating jobs that uphold the dignity and rights of workers—to productive work, to decent and just wages, to adequate benefits and security in their old age, to the choice of whether to organize and join unions, to the opportunity for legal status for immigrant workers, to private property, and to economic initiative. Workers also have responsibilities—to provide a fair day's work for a fair day's pay, to treat employers and co-workers with respect, and to carry out their work in ways that contribute to the common good. Workers, employers, and unions should not only advance their own interests, but also work together to advance economic justice and the well-being of all.

Solidarity

53. We are one human family, whatever our national, racial, ethnic, economic, and ideological differences. We are our brothers' and sisters' keepers, wherever they may be. Loving our neighbor has global dimensions and requires us to eradicate racism and address the extreme poverty and disease plaguing so much of the world.

Solidarity also includes the Scriptural call to welcome the stranger among us— including immigrants seeking work, a safe home, education for their children, and a decent life for their families. In light of the Gospel's invitation to be peacemakers, our commitment to solidarity with our neighbors—at home and abroad—also demands that we promote peace and pursue justice in a world marred by terrible violence and conflict. Decisions on the use of force should be guided by traditional moral criteria and undertaken only as a last resort. As Pope Paul VI taught: "If you want peace, work for justice" (*World Day of Peace Message*, January 1, 1972).

Caring for God's Creation

54. We show our respect for the Creator by our stewardship of God's creation. Care for the earth is a duty of our faith and a sign of our concern for all people. We should strive to live simply to meet the needs of the present without compromising the ability of future generations to meet their own needs. We have a moral obligation to protect the planet on which we live—to respect God's creation and to ensure a safe and hospitable environment for human beings, especially children at their most vulnerable stages of development. As stewards called by God to share the responsibility for the future of the earth, we should work for a world in which people respect and protect all of creation and seek to live simply in harmony with it for the sake of future generations.

55. These themes from Catholic social teaching provide a moral framework that does not easily fit ideologies of "right" or "left," "liberal" or "conservative," or the platform of any political party. They are not partisan or sectarian, but reflect fundamental ethical principles that are common to all people.

56. As leaders of the Church in the United States, we bishops have the duty to apply these moral principles to key public policy decisions facing our nation, outlining directions on issues that have important moral and ethical dimensions. More detailed information on policy directions adopted by our Bishops' Conference can be found in Part II of this document. We hope Catholics and others will seriously consider these policy applications as they make their own decisions in public life.

Conclusion

57. Building a world of respect for human life and dignity, where justice and peace prevail, requires more than just political commitment. Individuals, families, businesses, community organizations, and governments all have a role to play. Participation in political life in light of fundamental moral principles is an essential duty for every Catholic and all people of good will.

58. The Church is involved in the political process but is not partisan. The Church cannot champion any candidate or party. Our cause is the defense of human life and dignity and the protection of the weak and vulnerable.

59. The Church is engaged in the political process but should not be used. We welcome dialogue with political leaders and candidates; we seek to engage and persuade public officials. Events and "photo-ops" cannot substitute for serious dialogue.

60. The Church is principled but not ideological. We cannot compromise basic principles or moral teaching. We are committed to clarity about our moral teaching and to civility. In public life, it is important to practice the virtues of justice and charity that are at the core of our Tradition. We should work with others in a variety of ways to advance our moral principles.

61. In light of these principles and the blessings we share as part of a free and democratic nation, we bishops vigorously repeat our call for a renewed kind of politics:
- Focused more on moral principles than on the latest polls
- Focused more on the needs of the weak than on benefits for the strong
- Focused more on the pursuit of the common good than on the demands of narrow interests

62. This kind of political participation reflects the social teaching of our Church and the best traditions of our nation.

faithful citizenship

PART II

Applying Catholic Teaching to Major Issues: A Summary of Policy Positions of the United States Conference of Catholic Bishops

63. Politics is about values and issues as well as candidates and officeholders. In this brief summary, we bishops call attention to issues with significant moral dimensions that should be carefully considered in each campaign and as policy decisions are made in the years to come. As the descriptions below indicate, some issues involve principles that can never be violated, such as the fundamental right to life. Others reflect our judgment about the best way to apply Catholic principles to policy issues. No summary could fully reflect the depth and details of the positions taken through the work of the United States Conference of Catholic Bishops (USCCB). While people of good will may sometimes choose different ways to apply and act on some of our principles, Catholics cannot ignore their inescapable moral challenges or simply dismiss the Church's guidance or policy directions that flow from these principles. For a more complete review of these policy directions and their moral foundations, see the statements listed at the end of this document.

Human Life

64. Our 1998 statement *Living the Gospel of Life* declares, "**Abortion and euthanasia** have become preeminent threats to human life and dignity because they directly attack life itself, the most fundamental good and the condition for all others" (no. 5). **Abortion**, the deliberate killing of a human being before birth, is never morally acceptable and must always be opposed. **Cloning** and **destruction of human embryos** for research or even for potential cures are always wrong. The purposeful taking of human life by **assisted suicide and euthanasia** is not an act of mercy, but an unjustifiable assault on human life. **Genocide, torture,** and the **direct and intentional targeting of noncombatants in war or terrorist attacks** are always wrong.

19

65. Laws that legitimize any of these practices are profoundly unjust and immoral. Our Conference supports laws and policies to protect human life to the maximum degree possible, including constitutional protection for the unborn and legislative efforts to end abortion and euthanasia. We also promote a culture of life by supporting laws and programs that encourage childbirth and adoption over abortion and by addressing poverty, providing health care, and offering other assistance to pregnant women, children, and families.

66. The USCCB calls for greater assistance for those who are sick and dying, through health care for all and effective and compassionate palliative care. We recognize that addressing this complex issue effectively will require collaborative efforts between the public and private sectors and across party lines. Policies and decisions regarding **biotechnology** and human experimentation should respect the inherent dignity of human life from its very beginning, regardless of the circumstances of its origin. Respect for human life and dignity is also the foundation for essential efforts to address and overcome the hunger, disease, poverty, and violence that take the lives of so many innocent people.

67. Catholics must also work **to avoid war and to promote peace**. Nations should protect the dignity of the human person and the right to life by finding more effective ways to prevent conflicts, to resolve them by peaceful means, and to promote reconstruction and reconciliation in the wake of conflicts. Nations have a right and obligation to defend human life and the common good against terrorism, aggression, and similar threats. This duty demands effective responses to terror, moral assessment of and restraint in the means used, respect for ethical limits on the use of force, a focus on the roots of terror, and fair distribution of the burdens of responding to terror. The Church has raised fundamental moral concerns about **preventive use of military force**.[8] Our Church honors the commitment and sacrifice of those who serve in our nation's armed forces, and also recognizes the moral right to conscientious objection to war in general, a particular war, or a military procedure.

68. Even when military force can be justified as a last resort, it should not be indiscriminate or disproportionate. Direct and intentional attacks on noncombatants in war and terrorist acts are never morally acceptable. The use of weapons of mass destruction or other means of warfare that do not distinguish between civilians and soldiers is fundamentally immoral. The United States has a responsibility to work to reverse the spread of **nuclear, chemical, and biological weapons**, and to reduce its own reliance on weapons of mass destruction by pursuing progressive nuclear

disarmament. It also must end its use of anti-personnel landmines and reduce its predominant role in the global arms trade. The war in Iraq confronts us with urgent moral choices. We support a "responsible transition" that ends the war in a way that recognizes the continuing threat of fanatical extremism and global terror, minimizes the loss of life, and addresses the humanitarian crisis in Iraq, the refugee crisis in the region, and the need to protect human rights, especially religious freedom. This transition should reallocate resources from war to the urgent needs of the poor.

69. Society has a duty to defend life against violence and to reach out to victims of crime. Yet our nation's continued reliance on the **death penalty** cannot be justified. Because we have other ways to protect society that are more respectful of human life, the USCCB supports efforts to end the use of the death penalty and, in the meantime, to restrain its use through broader use of DNA evidence, access to effective counsel, and efforts to address unfairness and injustice related to application of the death penalty.

Family Life

70. The family is the basic cell of human society. The role, responsibilities, and needs of families should be central national priorities. **Marriage** must be defined, recognized, and protected as a lifelong commitment between a man and a woman, and as the source of the next generation and the protective haven for children. Policies on taxes, work, divorce, immigration, and welfare should help families stay together and should reward responsibility and sacrifice for children. **Wages** should allow workers to support their families, and public assistance should be available to help poor families to live in dignity. Such assistance should be provided in a manner that promotes eventual financial autonomy.

71. **Children** are to be valued, protected, and nurtured. As a Church, we affirm our commitment to the protection and well-being of children in our own institutions and in all of society. We oppose contraceptive mandates in public programs and health plans, which endanger rights of conscience and can interfere with parents' right to guide the moral formation of their children.

72. Parents—the first and most important educators—have a fundamental **right to choose the education** best suited to the needs of their children, including public, private, and religious schools. Government, through such means as tax credits and publicly funded scholarships, should help provide resources for parents, especially those of modest means, to exercise this basic right without discrimination. Students in all educational settings should have opportunities for moral and character formation.

73. Print, broadcast, and electronic **media** shape the culture. To protect children and families, responsible regulation is needed that respects freedom of speech yet also addresses policies that have lowered standards, permitted increasingly offensive material, and reduced opportunities for non-commercial religious programming.

74. Regulation should limit concentration of media control, resist management that is primarily focused on profit, and encourage a variety of program sources, including religious programming. TV rating systems and appropriate technology can assist parents in supervising what their children view.

75. The Internet offers both great benefits and significant problems. The benefits should be available to all students regardless of income. Because access to pornographic and violent material is becoming easier, vigorous enforcement of existing obscenity and child pornography laws is necessary, as well as technology that assists parents, schools, and libraries in blocking unwanted or undesirable materials.

Social Justice

76. Economic decisions and institutions should be assessed according to whether they protect or undermine the dignity of the human person. Social and economic policies should foster the creation of **jobs for all who can work** with decent working conditions and **just wages**. Barriers to equal pay and employment for

women and those facing unjust **discrimination must be overcome**. Catholic social teaching supports the **right of workers to choose whether to organize**, join a union, and bargain collectively, and to exercise these rights without reprisal. It also affirms **economic freedom, initiative, and the right to private property.** Workers, owners, employers, and unions should work together to create decent jobs, build a more just economy, and advance the common good.

77. **Welfare policy** should reduce **poverty** and dependency, strengthen family life, and help families leave poverty through work, training, and assistance with child care, health care, housing, and transportation. It should also provide a safety net for those who cannot work. Improving the **Earned Income Tax Credit** and **child tax credits**, available as refunds to families in greatest need, will help lift low-income families out of poverty.

78. **Faith-based groups** deserve recognition and support, not as a substitute for government, but as responsive, effective partners, especially in the poorest communities and countries. The USCCB actively supports conscience clauses, opposes any effort to undermine the ability of faith-based groups to preserve their identity and integrity as partners with government, and is committed to protecting long-standing civil rights and other protections for both religious groups and the people they serve. Government bodies should not require Catholic institutions to compromise their moral convictions to participate in government health or human service programs.

79. **Social Security** should provide adequate, continuing, and reliable income in an equitable manner for low- and average-wage workers and their families when these workers retire or become disabled, and for the survivors when a wage-earner dies.

80. **Affordable and accessible health care** is an essential safeguard of human life and a fundamental human right. With an estimated 47 million Americans lacking health care coverage, it is also an urgent national priority. Reform of the nation's health care system needs to be rooted in values that respect human dignity, protect human life, and meet the needs of the poor and uninsured, especially born and unborn children, pregnant women, immigrants, and other vulnerable populations. Religious groups should be able to provide health care without compromising their religious convictions. The USCCB supports measures to strengthen Medicare and Medicaid. Our Conference also advocates effective, compassionate care that reflects Catholic moral values for those suffering from HIV/AIDS and those coping with addictions.

81. The lack of safe, affordable **housing** requires a renewed commitment to increase the supply of quality housing and to preserve, maintain, and improve existing housing through public/private partnerships, especially with religious groups and community organizations. The USCCB continues to oppose unjust housing discrimination and to support measures to meet the credit needs of low-income and minority communities.

82. A first priority for **agriculture** policy should be **food security for all**. Because no one should face **hunger** in a land of plenty, Food Stamps, the Special Nutrition Program for Women, Infants, and Children (WIC), and other nutrition programs need to be strong and effective. Farmers and farm workers who grow, harvest, and process food deserve a just return for their labor, with safe and just working conditions and adequate housing. Supporting rural communities sustains a way of life that enriches our nation. Careful stewardship of the earth and its natural resources demands policies that support **sustainable agriculture** as vital elements of agricultural policy.

83. The Gospel mandate to "welcome the stranger" requires Catholics to care for and stand with **immigrants**, both documented and undocumented, including

immigrant children. Comprehensive reform is urgently necessary to fix a broken immigration system and should include a temporary work program with worker protections and a path to permanent residency; family reunification policies; a broad and fair legalization program; access to legal protections, including due process and essential public programs; refuge for those fleeing persecution and exploitation; and policies to address the root causes of migration. The right and responsibility of nations to control their borders and to maintain the rule of law should be recognized.

84. All persons have a right to receive a quality **education**. Young people, including those who are poor and those with disabilities, need to have the opportunity to develop intellectually, morally, spiritually, and physically, allowing them to become good citizens who make socially and morally responsible decisions. This requires parental choice in education. It also requires educational institutions to have orderly, just, respectful, and non-violent environments where adequate professional and material resources are available. The USCCB strongly supports adequate funding, including scholarships, tax credits, and other means, to educate all persons no matter what their personal condition or what school they attend—public, private, or religious. All teachers and administrators deserve salaries and benefits that reflect principles of economic justice, as well as access to resources necessary for teachers to prepare for their important tasks. Services aimed at improving education—especially for those most at risk—that are available to students and teachers in public schools should also be available to students and teachers in **private and religious schools** as a matter of justice.

85. Promoting moral responsibility and effective responses to violent crime, curbing violence in media, supporting reasonable restrictions on access to assault weapons and handguns, and opposing the use of the **death penalty** are particularly important in light of a growing "culture of violence." An ethic of responsibility, rehabilitation, and restoration should be a foundation for the reform of our broken **criminal justice system**. A remedial, rather than a strictly punitive, approach to offenders should be developed.

86. It is important for our society to continue to combat **discrimination** based on race, religion, sex, ethnicity, disabling condition, or age, as these are grave injustices and affronts to human dignity. Where the effects of past discrimination persist, society has the obligation to take positive steps to overcome the legacy of injustice, including vigorous action to remove barriers to education and equal employment for women and minorities.

87. **Care for the earth** and for the environment is a moral issue. Protecting the land, water, and air we share is a religious duty of stewardship and reflects our responsibility to born and unborn children, who are most vulnerable to environmental assault. Effective initiatives are required for energy conservation and the development of alternate, renewable, and clean-energy resources. Our Conference offers a distinctive call to seriously address **global climate change**, focusing on the virtue of prudence, pursuit of the common good, and the impact on the poor, particularly on vulnerable workers and the poorest nations. The United States should lead in contributing to the sustainable development of poorer nations and promoting greater justice in sharing the burden of environmental blight, neglect, and recovery.

Global Solidarity

88. A more just world will likely be a more peaceful world, a world less vulnerable to terrorism and other violence. The United States has the responsibility to take the lead in addressing the scandal of **poverty and underdevelopment.** Our nation should help to **humanize globalization**, addressing its negative consequences and spreading its benefits, especially among the world's poor. The United States also has a unique opportunity to use its power in partnership with others to build a more just and peaceful world.

- The United States should take a leading role in helping to **alleviate global poverty** through substantially increased development aid for the poorest countries, more equitable trade policies, and continuing efforts to relieve the crushing burdens of debt and disease. Our nation's efforts to reduce poverty should not be associated with demeaning and sometimes coercive population control programs; instead, these efforts should focus on working with the poor to help them build a future of hope and opportunity for themselves and their children.

- U.S. policy should promote **religious liberty** and other basic **human rights**. The use of **torture** must be rejected as fundamentally incompatible with the dignity of the human person and ultimately counterproductive in the effort to combat terrorism.

- The United States should provide political and financial support for beneficial **United Nations** programs and reforms, for other **international bodies**, and for international law, so that together these institutions may become more responsible and responsive agents for addressing global problems.

- Asylum should be afforded to refugees who hold a well-founded fear of persecution in their homelands. Our country should support protection for **persons fleeing persecution** through safe haven in other countries, including the United States, especially for unaccompanied children, women, victims of human trafficking, and religious minorities.

- Our country should be a leader—in collaboration with the international community—in addressing **regional conflicts** in the Middle East, the Balkans, the Congo, Sudan, Colombia, and West Africa.

- Leadership on the **Israeli-Palestinian conflict** is an especially urgent priority. The United States should actively pursue comprehensive negotiations leading to a just and peaceful resolution that respects the legitimate claims and aspirations of both Israelis and Palestinians, ensuring security for Israel, a viable state for Palestinians, respect for Lebanon's sovereignty, and peace in the region.

- While the Holy See and our Conference have raised serious moral questions regarding the war in Iraq, as bishops we urgently call on our country to work with the international community to seek a "responsible transition" in Iraq and to address the human consequences of war in **Iraq and Afghanistan**.

Defending human life, building peace, combating poverty and despair, and protecting freedom and human rights are not only moral imperatives—they are wise national priorities that will make our nation and world safer.

PART III

Goals for Political Life:
Challenges for Citizens,
Candidates, and Public Officials

89. As Catholics, we are led to raise questions for political life other than "Are you better off than you were two or four years ago?" Our focus is not on party affiliation, ideology, economics, or even competence and capacity to perform duties, as important as such issues are. Rather, we focus on what protects or threatens human life and dignity.

90. Catholic teaching challenges voters and candidates, citizens and elected officials, to consider the moral and ethical dimensions of public policy issues. In light of ethical principles, we bishops offer the following policy goals that we hope will guide Catholics as they form their consciences and reflect on the moral dimensions of their public choices. Not all issues are equal; these ten goals address matters of different moral weight and urgency. Some involve matters of intrinsic evil that can never be supported. Others involve affirmative obligations to seek the common good. These and similar goals can help voters and candidates act on ethical principles rather than particular interests and partisan allegiances. We hope Catholics will ask candidates how they intend to help our nation pursue these important goals:

- Address the preeminent requirement to protect the weakest in our midst—innocent unborn children—by restricting and bringing to an end the destruction of unborn children through abortion.

29

- Keep our nation from turning to violence to address fundamental problems—a million abortions each year to deal with unwanted pregnancies, euthanasia and assisted suicide to deal with the burdens of illness and disability, the destruction of human embryos in the name of research, the use of the death penalty to combat crime, and imprudent resort to war to address international disputes.

- Define the central institution of marriage as a union between one man and one woman, and provide better support for family life morally, socially, and economically, so that our nation helps parents raise their children with respect for life, sound moral values, and an ethic of stewardship and responsibility.

- Achieve comprehensive immigration reform that secures our borders, treats immigrant workers fairly, offers an earned path to citizenship, respects the rule of law, and addresses the factors that compel people to leave their own countries.

- Help families and children overcome poverty: ensuring access to and choice in education, as well as decent work at fair, living wages and adequate assistance for the vulnerable in our nation, while also helping to overcome widespread hunger and poverty around the world, especially in the areas of development assistance, debt relief, and international trade.

- Provide health care for the growing number of people without it, while respecting human life, human dignity, and religious freedom in our health care system.

- Continue to oppose policies that reflect prejudice, hostility toward immigrants, religious bigotry, and other forms of discrimination.

- Encourage families, community groups, economic structures, and government to work together to overcome poverty, pursue the common good, and care for creation, with full respect for religious groups and their right to address social needs in accord with their basic moral convictions.

- Establish and comply with moral limits on the use of military force—examining for what purposes it may be used, under what authority, and at what human cost—and work for a "responsible transition" to end the war in Iraq.

- Join with others around the world to pursue peace, protect human rights and religious liberty, and advance economic justice and care for creation.

Notes

1   The common good is "the sum total of social conditions which allow people, either as groups or as individuals, to reach their fulfillment more fully and more easily" (*Catechism of the Catholic Church*, no. 1906).

2   "Ignorance of Christ and his Gospel, bad example given by others, enslavement to one's passions, assertion of a mistaken notion of autonomy of conscience, rejection of the Church's authority and her teaching, lack of conversion and charity: these can be at the source of errors of judgment in moral conduct" (*Catechism of the Catholic Church*, no. 1792).

3   "When political activity comes up against moral principles that do not admit of exception, compromise, or derogation, the Catholic commitment becomes more evident and laden with responsibility. In the face of *fundamental and inalienable ethical demands*, Christians must recognize that what is at stake is the essence of the moral law, which concerns the integral good of the human person. This is the case with laws concerning *abortion* and *euthanasia*. . . . Such laws must defend the basic right to life from conception to natural death" (*Doctrinal Note on Some Questions Regarding the Participation of Catholics in Political Life*, no. 4).

4   See *Catechism of the Catholic Church*, no. 2297.

5   For statements from the bishops of the United States on Catholics serving in public life and on the reception of Holy Communion, see *Catholics in Political Life* (2004) and *Happy Are Those Who Are Called to His Supper: On Preparing to Receive Christ Worthily in the Eucharist* (2006).

6   These themes are drawn from a rich tradition of principles and ideas that are more fully described in the *Compendium of the Social Doctrine of the Church* from the Pontifical Council for Justice and Peace (Washington, DC: United States Conference of Catholic Bishops, 2005).

7   See *Catechism of the Catholic Church*, no. 2297.

8   See *Compendium of the Social Doctrine of the Church*, no. 501.

References

Catechism of the Catholic Church (2nd ed.). Washington, DC: Libreria Editrice Vaticana—United States Conference of Catholic Bishops (USCCB), 2000.

Congregation for the Doctrine of the Faith. *Doctrinal Note on Some Questions Regarding the Participation of Catholics in Political Life.* In *Readings on Catholics in Political Life*. Washington, DC: USCCB, 2006.

Pope Benedict XVI. *Deus Caritas Est (God Is Love)*. Washington, DC: USCCB, 2006.

Pope Benedict XVI. *Sacramentum Caritatis (The Sacrament of Charity)*. Washington, DC: USCCB, 2007.

Pope John XXIII. *Pacem in Terris (Peace on Earth)*. Washington, DC: USCCB, 1963.

Pope John Paul II. *Christifideles Laici (On the Vocation and the Mission of the Lay Faithful in the Church and in the World)*. Washington, DC: USCCB, 1989.

Pope John Paul II. *Evangelium Vitae (The Gospel of Life)*. Washington, DC: USCCB, 1995.

Pope John Paul II. *Veritatis Splendor (The Splendor of Truth)*. Washington, DC: USCCB, 1993.

Second Vatican Council. *Dignitatis Humanae (Declaration on Religious Liberty)*. In *Vatican Council II: Volume 1: The Conciliar and Post Conciliar Documents*. Edited by Austin Flannery. Northport, NY: Costello Publishing, 1996.

Second Vatican Council. *Gaudium et Spes (Pastoral Constitution on the Church in the Modern World)*. In *Vatican Council II: Volume 1: The Conciliar and Post Conciliar Documents*. Edited by Austin Flannery. Northport, NY: Costello Publishing, 1996.

USCCB. *Living the Gospel of Life: A Challenge to American Catholics*. Washington, DC: USCCB, 1998.

Major Catholic Statements on Public Life and Moral Issues

The following documents from the United States Conference of Catholic Bishops (USCCB) explore in greater detail the public policy issues discussed in *Forming Consciences for Faithful Citizenship*. Under some of the headings, documents are grouped generally by topic and then by year.

For more information on these and other documents, visit the USCCB Web site: *www.usccb.org*. Documents marked with an asterisk are not available online.

Protecting Human Life

A Matter of the Heart: A Statement on the Thirtieth Anniversary of Roe v. Wade, 2002 (*www.usccb.org/prolife/heart.shtml*)

Pastoral Plan for Pro-Life Activities: A Campaign in Support of Life, 2001 (*www.usccb.org/prolife/pastoralplan.shtml*)

Living the Gospel of Life: A Challenge to American Catholics, 1998 (*www.usccb.org/ prolife/gospel.shtml*)

Faithful for Life: A Moral Reflection, 1995 (*www.usccb.org/prolife/tdocs/ FaithfulForLife.pdf*)

Resolution on Abortion, 1989 (*www.usccb.org/prolife/tdocs/resabort89.shtml*)

Documentation on the Right to Life and Abortion, 1974, 1976, 1981*

Statement on Iraq, 2002 (*www.usccb.org/bishops/iraq.shtml*)

A Pastoral Message: Living with Faith and Hope After September 11, 2001 (*www.usccb.org/sdwp/sept11.shtml*)

Sowing the Weapons of War, 1995 (*www.usccb.org/sdwp/international/ weaponsofwar.shtml*)

The Harvest of Justice Is Sown in Peace, 1993 (*www.usccb.org/sdwp/harvest.shtml*)

A Report on the Challenge of Peace and Policy Developments, 1983-1888, 1989*

The Challenge of Peace: God's Promise and Our Response, 1983 (*www.usccb.org/ sdwp/international/TheChallengeofPeace.pdf*)

Welcome and Justice for Persons with Disabilities, 1999 (*www.usccb.org/doctrine/disabilities.htm*)

Nutrition and Hydration: Moral and Pastoral Reflections, 1992 (*www.usccb.org/prolife/issues/euthanas/nutindex.shtml*)

Statement on Euthanasia, 1991 (*www.usccb.org/prolife/issues/euthanas/euthnccb.shtml*)

Pastoral Statement of U.S. Catholic Bishops on Persons with Disabilities, 1984 (*www.ncpd.org/pastoral_statement_1978.htm*)

A Culture of Life and the Penalty of Death, 2005 (*www.usccb.org/sdwp/national/penaltyofdeath.pdf*)

Confronting a Culture of Violence, 1995 (*www.usccb.org/sdwp/national/criminal/ccv94.shtml*)

Statement on Capital Punishment, 1980 (*www.usccb.org/sdwp/national/criminal/death/uscc80.shtml*)

Promoting Family Life

National Directory for Catechesis, 2005 (*www.usccb.org/education/ndc/index.shtml*)

Renewing Our Commitment to Catholic Elementary and Secondary Schools in the Third Millennium, 2005 (*www.usccb.org/bishops/schools.pdf*)

Sharing Catholic Social Teaching: Challenges and Directions, 1998 (*www.usccb.org/sdwp/projects/socialteaching/socialteaching.shtml*)

Principles for Educational Reform in the United States, 1995 (*www.usccb.org/education/parentassn/reform.shtml*)

To Teach as Jesus Did: A Pastoral Message on Catholic Education, 1972*

When I Call for Help: A Pastoral Response to Domestic Violence Against Women, 2002 (*www.usccb.org/laity/help.shtml*)

A Family Perspective in Church and Society, 1998 (*www.usccb.org/laity/marriage/family.shtml*)

Blessings of Age, 1999 (*www.usccb.org/laity/blessings*)

Between Man and Woman: Questions and Answers About Marriage and Same-Sex Unions, 2003 (*www.usccb.org/laity/manandwoman.shtml*)

Walk in the Light: A Pastoral Response to Child Sexual Abuse, 1995 (*www.usccb.org/ laity/walk.shtml*)

Follow the Way of Love: A Pastoral Message to Families, 1993 (*www.usccb.org/ laity/follow.shtml*)

Putting Children and Families First: A Challenge for Our Church, Nation and World, 1992*

Pursuing Social Justice

"For I Was Hungry and You Gave Me Food": Catholic Reflections on Food, Farmers and Farmworkers, 2003 (*www.usccb.org/bishops/agricultural.shtml*)

Strangers No Longer: Together on the Journey of Hope, 2003 (*www.usccb.org/mrs/ stranger.shtml*)

A Place at the Table: A Catholic Recommitment to Overcome Poverty and to Respect the Dignity of All God's Children, 2002 (*www.usccb.org/bishops/table.shtml*)

Ethical and Religious Directives for Catholic Health Care Services (Fourth Edition), 2001 (*www.usccb.org/bishops/directives.shtml*)

Global Climate Change: A Plea for Dialogue, Prudence, and the Common Good, 2001 (*www.usccb.org/sdwp/international/globalclimate.shtml*)

Responsibility, Rehabilitation, and Restoration: A Catholic Perspective on Crime and Criminal Justice, 2000 (*www.usccb.org/sdwp/criminal.shtml*)

A Commitment to All Generations: Social Security and the Common Good, 1999 (*www.usccb.org/sdwp/national/commitment.shtml*)

In All Things Charity: A Pastoral Challenge for the New Millennium, 1999 (*www.usccb.org/cchd/charity.shtml*)

One Family Under God, 1995*

Confronting a Culture of Violence: A Catholic Framework for Action, 1995 (*www.usccb.org/sdwp/national/criminal/ccv94.shtml*)

Moral Principles and Policy Priorities for Welfare Reform, 1995*

The Harvest of Justice Is Sown in Peace, 1993 (*www.usccb.org/sdwp/harvest.shtml*)

A Framework for Comprehensive Health Care Reform, 1993*

Renewing the Earth: An Invitation to Reflection and Action on the Environment in Light of Catholic Social Teaching, 1992 (www.usccb.org/sdwp/ejp/bishopsstatement.shtml)

Putting Children and Families First: A Challenge for Our Church, Nation and World, 1992*

New Slavery, New Freedom: A Pastoral Message on Substance Abuse, 1990*

Brothers and Sisters to Us: Pastoral Letter on Racism in Our Day, 1989 (www.usccb.org/saac/bishopspastoral.shtml)

Called to Compassion and Responsibility: A Response to the HIV/AIDS Crisis, 1989 (www.usccb.org/sdwp/international/ctoresp.shtml)

Homelessness and Housing: A Human Tragedy, A Moral Challenge, 1988*

Economic Justice for All, 1986 (www.usccb.org/sdwp/international/EconomicJusticeforAll.pdf)

Practicing Global Solidarity

A Call to Solidarity with Africa, 2001 (www.usccb.org/sdwp/africa.shtml)

A Jubilee Call for Debt Forgiveness, 1999 (www.usccb.org/sdwp/international/adminstm.shtml)

Called to Global Solidarity: International Challenges for U.S. Parishes, 1998 (www.usccb.org/sdwp/international/globalsolidarity.shtml)

Sowing the Weapons of War, 1995 (www.usccb.org/sdwp/international/weaponsofwar.shtml)

One Family Under God, 1995*

The Harvest of Justice Is Sown in Peace, 1993 (www.usccb.org/sdwp/harvest.shtml)

The New Moment in Eastern and Central Europe, 1990*

Toward Peace in the Middle East, 1989 (www.usccb.org/sdwp/international/TowardPeaceintheMiddleEast.pdf)

Statement on Central America, 1987 (www.usccb.org/sdwp/international/cenamst.shtml)